FROM THE
INSIDE OUT

R. STEVEN HOLMES

Studio Griffin
A Publishing Company
www.studiogriffin.net

For information, contact:
Studio Griffin
A Publishing Company
studiogriffin@outlook.com
www.studiogriffin.net

Cover Design by R. Steven Holmes
Photographs by © Cedric Van Buren of Van Buren Photography
Images generated with the assistance of AI

First Edition

ISBN-13: 978-1-954818-44-6

Library of Congress Control Number: 2024900268

1 2 3 4 5 6 7 8 9 10

This book is dedicated to my foundation... my family.

To my parents Moses and Mattie Holmes, I could not have done this without you.

Dad, you went to a better place on October 24, 2022. Through all my years of ups and downs, you never once looked down on me. This is the first time I pray that you are. You will always be my rock and inspiration. I thank you for the strength that you instilled in me and all the positive words and support you gave me over the years. You are missed and I love you!

To my Mom, words can't express the person and personality you are. You are comfort, you are laughter and most of all, you are love. Thank you for your unrequited love and nurturing. Your commitment to your family can never be repaid.

To my sisters Anecia and Sabrina, know that I always wanted a brother! Also know that I would not trade the two of you for anything! Having two sisters taught me how to appreciate and value women. I thank you for allowing me to be a playmate and a protector, all at the same time. Our bonds will always be special.

To my sons Tyson Holmes and Mykael Cooper. The two of you changed my life. You taught me that value is not monetary but something physical and mental. Everything I do is for you! I'm so honored to be your Dad and Father.

To my wife Monique Turrentine Holmes. Without you, this book would not have been written. Thank you for loving me in a way I wasn't used to. You push me when I need to be pushed and pull me when I shouldn't be heading in a certain direction. For all the nights you endured my journey and fell asleep listening to me read to you, I thank you for caring. Thank you for always being by my side ready to take on the world with me.

To all my nieces and nephews who have given me inspiration, I hope I'm always your favorite 'Uncle Steve.'

Thank you to my extended family. I can only hope that I make you proud.

TABLE OF CONTENTS

PREFACE

In my early years, I observed the actions and habits of the people around me. I was highly intrigued and heavily influenced by sports and music. Like most kids growing up in the 80s, I wanted to be an athlete or a rapper. Interestingly enough, I did both. While attending East Carolina University, I was a member of the Pirates football team and explored a brief rap career upon graduation. While juggling my passions, I developed a love for writing more than just rap verses. I began writing for a campus magazine and sharing some of my personal writings in the publication. It was then I began to realize and understand the power of words and how they stood on their own without music.

My poetry was different, and I embraced that. As years passed, I shared my writings in newspapers and other media outlets. As social media began to heighten, I saw this as a prime tool to express the things that were going on inside of me. As my life evolved from being single, to married, to father, to divorced, I shared more and more of my writings on the various social media platforms.

In this book of poems, you will experience the different phases that were occurring in my life. A young boy that aspired to be a star athlete to becoming a young man battling anger and anxiety. The progression throughout this book chronicles my thoughts and journey to finding peace and happiness as an adult.

FORWARD: THE JOURNEY

There was a time when all I cared about on social media was impressing the stray 'passer-byers' who were viewing my Facebook or Instagram pages. Whether it was actual facts or embellished rhetoric, my purpose for posting was to say, *"Hey, I got that too,"* or *"I can do that also!"* I was on a mission to hide every struggle I was going through. That mission was to seek, destroy and cloud the views of everyone who thought and believed I would fail or not rise from my struggles to be what THEY thought I should be. The oxymoron, outside of me being a complete moron, was that not many people knew my struggles. I had mastered being the rock for so many other people, that no one knew when I also needed a rock to lean on, rest on or hold me upright. I was there to give advice and offer help to anyone who needed or asked for it. That's how I was raised and how I've always been.

Through that season of my life, I found that not everyone shared my views and upbringing regarding friendship. Not everyone had the kind heart that I had. Not everyone cared about my struggles. I noticed people only circled my page like vultures when there was an aroma of a fresh meal to come. I was on the verge of depression and self-doubt. Through it all, I remained the person whom people thought I was on the outside, while I lied to myself and was slowly dying on the inside. Constant trips to the doctor, body deteriorating, weight gain, anxiety… the list of ailments was growing and growing. I turned to God and family because I knew my sons needed me. Truthfully, I felt they needed me here more than I wanted to be here myself.

I constantly summoned the competitive spirit inside of me just to get up every day and make it into the night. I challenged myself to be stronger and to be better than the day before. I went to work like normal, went out in public like normal, but when I was at home, NOTHING about me was normal. I poured more love into my sons knowing that their love was in its purest form. I constantly repeated in my head that love isn't love until you give it away, hoping that the same form of love would be returned to me by the ones I felt turned their backs on me in my time of need.

Self-reflection and studying myself lead me to know that not everyone wants to see you succeed. Some are just there to admire your gifts long enough to steal them away when you least expect it. Some are close to you to simply be an eyewitness of your demise. My deep look in the mirror showed me my flaws as I asked over and over again, "Why would anyone want to take from me or envy anything about this life I live?" It was the constant questioning of myself that allowed me to receive every answer I sought out.

Man will fail you time and time again. We are ALL flawed. They may come from the same tree but grow their branches differently. The flaws in others were not for me to understand or try to cure. I first needed to address my own. Pulling away was the only alternative for me to eventually reconnect with the ones who were truly there for me to plug into. I first needed to water my own seeds and strengthen my own roots in order to grow.

The self-doubt slowly began to fade away. I was no longer questioning the things I used to. I shined light into the dark cloud of, "If only they knew what I was going through," because in reality, they didn't. I took my imaginary straw and sucked out all the negativity that haloed my existence. Soon my halo started to take on a new form and a new luster. And although the competitive nature within me still runs rampant inside, I was able to laugh in the presence of competition and say to myself, "If you only knew! And through every struggle and trial that came before me... I Am Still Here!"

Poetry was my escape from the world to create a canvas to paint my own story and discover who I was again... From the Inside Out!

MY LIFE

I woke up this morning and looked around.
The Sun was rising, the birds were singing, a deep breath fills
my lungs.
The burn from early morning eyes is replaced by the sight of a
cool blue sky.
My senses are refreshed as warm water rains gently upon my
flesh.

I AM ALIVE!

I entered the world this afternoon.
Cars darted and swerved in anxious anticipation of an
unwanted destination.
Eyes turn red in anger as Competition and Jealousy enter the
building.
Innocent children await the fate of a guilty parent's failure.
Hearts grow heavy and heads bow down in regret of past
decisions.
The Sun sets...
A car is stolen, a child is killed.
Another man is falsely accused, another fatherless child.
Impurities travel through the youthful bodies of would be
'superstars.'
Night falls...
Heaviness fills my eyes.
My body relaxes.
A deep breath fills my lungs.
My heartbeat is nothing more than a gentle tapping motion
within my shell.

I AM AT REST!

Tomorrow comes again.

DIARY

This is just a sample,
it's been a long time,
since I mixed my emotions
with poetic lines of rhyme...

I do this for the therapy
to release the stress,
when the pain hits my chest
like bullets without the vest...

I nestle down in my word,
mix my actions with verbs,
and exhale the next tale,
hoping the message is heard...

It's been a rough two years
but this is Steve now,
shed some tears, buried fears
wear my heart on my sleeve now...

Feeling replenished and stronger,
this is like my diary,
ripping pages from the spine
hoping the fallout inspires me...

Oh, how they hate to admire me
so I juggled my circles,
never knew so many woke up
just plotting to hurt you...

Had to change the game plan
to be a better man,
told God I ain't to blame
but I'll try to be a better fan...

Seasons came, status changed,
single and filled with prayer now,
never fell off my game
so, I guess I'm a player now?

Just a day in the life,
fighting perception without a weapon,
like walking on hot coals
I turned cold and kept stepping...

People always ask the question
"What were you talking about?"
Well, I get filled sometimes
I just have to pour it out...

So, I let it spill on the paper,
give you the key to the vault,
expose my open wounds,
hoping you don't have salt...

Can't spend my life ducking shade
or anticipating the rain,
even through cloudy weather
when the sun shines I gain...

Hard to understand
why people are so needy,
stealing pages from my book
so, I closed it and stopped reading...

Started a new chapter
with better characters to capture,
separated from the fiction
got new journeys to master...

And learn my lessons through confessions,
knowing you gotta be true,
and realize people hate
because they wanna be you...

CHOCOLATE PUDDIN'

A creamy brown mixture of wetness and pleasure…

Warm or cold, it is complete satisfaction!

So soft and wet as it slides across my tongue,
creating desires to devour my chocolate passion…

I am playful as I experience my chocolate dish.
Spreading its smoothness upon my lips,
only to anxiously remove its taste with quick palpitations of
my tongue…

Soon I am engulfed in chocolate delight!

My tongue is fully submerged within the depths of a chocolate
wave,
having the intent to explore every taste and every surprise…

At last, I reach the bottom of this chocolate voyage…

An explosion of fulfilling sensations overtake my body…

My spoon rings around the rim of what used to hold my
chocolate ecstasy…

As I look on, my mouth waters and my mind flashes back to
my experience of a true chocolate paradise…

Chocolate Puddin'…

Mounds of chocolatey dreams...
The pleasure of bodily satisfaction...
The mind stimulating experience of total relaxation...

AND most of all...

The promising revelation that seconds are only seconds away!

FUNNY LOVE

It's funny how life can change in the blink of eye,
how things can be so sweet,
then all of a sudden
you're THAT guy …

The one who makes mistakes,
the one who takes the fall,
the one who's full of pride
then has no pride at all…

It's funny how people
can change like the wind,
leave you not knowing where love stops
and where hate begins…

It's funny how people judge
but hate to be judged,
how people say they're making progress
but haven't ever budged…

It's funny how emotions
come and go in seconds,
And in a second,
your actions can take a life and wreck it…

Funny how a door can open and close so fast,
with your future on one side
and in your present, your past…

But it's times like this,
you have to trust in yourself,
And treat love like money
and invest in your wealth...

Life has to be a game
because we know games aren't real,
so, this has to be a game of cards,
from the hand life deals...

And the pain that is felt
is just a harder mode,
and the love that is missing,
we haven't unlocked the code...

It's funny, so funny
how love can be,
but when love is funny, it's not funny to me...

STRESS-FILLED QUEST

Stress fills my chest
like Buddha Bless fills a junkie,
curious for facts
like that yellow-hatted man and his monkey...

But love becomes me
as I await the pearly gates,
with two crates carrying my fate
and dead weight around my waist...

I waste not the moment,
the key to life I've been shown it,
an honest man in the Promised Land
I'll throw these hands and I own it...

It's like I have to box demons
to beat the allegiance of treason,
giving ninety-nine reasons to choose my mind over my
semen...

Constantly bleeding,
spilling my talents from a King's chalice,
to breed a spectacular being
housing a heart without malice...

But that's the greatest challenge
they often take me for granted,
tears from forty plus years
have watered these roots that are planted...

Fantasizing about needs,
seeds to build this tree of chemistry,
with rotted branches or three chances
and that's what limits me...

A bunch of projects without logic
and misogynistic garbage,
keeps my brain cluttered and full,
I can't fall forward for yardage...

And when the day ends, I'm still stressed,
CHANGE has again outrun my desire,
on higher ground but still drowning
that's how the mind forces you to retire...

IN DUE TIME...

Breath in... Breath out...
just keep breathing,
the more I inhale,
the more air that keeps leaving...

Until I'm heaving,
I feel queasy,
these butterflies won't leave me,
death is not an option,
God, you know my son needs me...

Palms start to sweat
my knees knock together,
redirect your thoughts,
that's supposed to make you feel
better...

Since I love my music
I play it to rest,
but I can't sleep with the Little Drummer Boy
beating in my chest...

Heart pounding... Cold sweats,
I just wanna sleep,
how can someone strong as me
constantly feel so weak...

Anxiety ain't for the meek
It's been almost ten years now,

I rejoice when I awake,
although I don't know how...

Every day is a battle
but I will not be depressed,
I just try to live peaceful
while my body thinks I'm stressed...

Sometimes I feel possessed,
every thought I think twice,
and while I'm suppressing aggression
people say I'm too nice...

But if you only knew
how I've programmed myself,
I use creative outlets,
you think I do it for the wealth...

I do it for the release,
I don't care what people say,
the doctor gave me meds,
the Pastor told me to pray...

And I pray for me
but I still care too much,
so I prayed that when you cross me
you won't have to feel my touch...

Trust is the issue,
I've contemplated and hate it,
I've tried to take this broken glass,
stain it and create a mosaic...

Be mindful, be alert

but none of that works,
my alter ego is Hulk strong
and that's the part that hurts worse...

I hate the way it makes me feel,
it makes me feel defeated,
I've never faced something I've studied
and still feel I can't beat it...

It's weakened my pride
but I've never been one to boast,
because I've learned,
it's the wounds you can't see
that hurt you the most...

My friends call me for advice
so I put on my act,
but when it's my turn to speak,
they never call back...

I've given all of me too much
time and time again,
while I vibe of that saying
'Check on your strong friends...'

But that's my nature,
I've never had regrets,
except waking in the mornings
to sheets wet with sweat...

And not knowing the cause,
pressure gets the best of me,
that's why it took years
to trust the person lying next to me...

I panic, but never frantic,
my alter ego is kinda weird,
It's like a rush of adrenaline
but this excitement is to be feared...

But fear is for the weak
strength comes from the mind,
check the clock, you're my witness
Joy comes in due time!

TRUTH HURTS

Everything's about money,
Keto diet... you should try it,
but they lying,
it only decreases pounds
because you're buying ...

Into money schemes,
the emotional motion
of drama means,
we have no relevance
unless we know what the comma brings...

Pause... let it sink it,
6 figures... I left the link in the description,
watch how many clicks it gets
before you mention...

My name
you stole my history to make a claim
but you never thought to alter,
so come get rocked with us like Gibraltar...

The walls WILL fall down
with Jeri co-existing in the distance,
and Imma still be watching,
still scrolling through my shit list...

My senses get no emphasis,
my feelings get no attention,

until I bug out and Raid your space,
refer back to the aforementioned...

You're really just mad
because I go against the normal,
well, I'm sorry to inform you,
I ain't never been that formal...

My DNA won't clone
to whoever you thought I could be,
two teams playing tug of war
for who they thought I should be...

A simple man
facing unrealistic demands,
at the hands of overthinking
on my heels to understand...

Branded with an iron,
frying panoramic images into my brain,
the main thing is to maintain
the very thing that brings pain...

How twisted the thought
that brought light once before,
to have foundation but desire
what's behind another's door...

Separation can bring depression,
leave you in the sunken place,
drunken monkey face flailing,
failing to let the sun replace...

All internal darkness,
middle child now middle-aged,
trying to bridge the Gap
Outstanding but in a cage...

Through a checkerboard view
I remain thought-provoking,
dodging ejaculating egos
in other words,
a lot of stroking...

Choking down hate,
absorbing heat in my Black state,
no reflection but the mirror
still mocks me with Black face...

No debate, no trolling,
game of life bowling with boulders,
dodging LIES in the gutter
with Sojourner TRUTH over my shoulder...

3AM SOCIAL MEDIA DRIVE-BY

You went from fat to fine,
now no one can stand you,
spray tans and brands,
always wondering what a man do …

Let me post this pic
to see how many clicks I can get,
then call them all thirsty
for looking at my tits…

My self-esteem is a dream
that I'm trying to achieve,
Snap… post another selfie,
This'll make them believe…

That I'm happy, I'm fit,
I'm 2 legit 2 quit,
I'll bait them all in
then I'll treat'em like shit…

I'll call them dead beats
who can't handle me,
and while I know who I want,
I'll date randomly …

I'm too strong for the average,
So, I'll just dream about marriage,
I have the power of a horse,
I just don't have the carriage…

I'll speak of a man
but I won't show his face,
that'll surely attract more people
to fill up my space...

How can someone so fine
be single as f*ck,
I'll catch'em in my inbox
'cause I don't mingle that much...

Went from fit teas to dancer,
Aquarius to Cancer,
greatest love... your kids,
grown men don't get a chance to...

Love you or leave you
while you just self promote,
and place all your value
in likes and emotes...

Snap... 'Doing me!!'
but we all see the trap,
I'll just look through these binoculars,
I'm not giving you any dap...

"Why should I look in the mirror?"
"I'd rather use my phone,"
yes, we see all your selfies
we also see you're alone!

SMOKE & FIRE

I can't tell
who's with me or against me,
I saw the shots fired and
all I know is they missed me...

But I see you my brotha
and I see your gun still smoking,
bumping elbows with the fellows
but smiling like you're joking...

While your words keep provoking
me - to get my story and tell it,
funny how people talk so much shit
but claim they can't smell it...

When it's right under their nose
but I suppose that's your clue,
most don't talk about shit
when they're standing next to you...

I'm just trying to be a man,
you can be a man too,
ran through your thoughts
and disMANtled
your mental dandruff like shampoo...

Damn you,
haters and debaters,
killing my daily high deflaters,

you can't block my success,
hear me now or feel me later...

Ain't no crater or valley
keeping me from the creator,
never hide but hard to find
if you don't pull back the layers...

My mind is outside the box
like Pop Rocks and soda,
raining down tears
from the tiers of my pagoda...

I know you smell the aroma,
my blood, sweat and tears,
carrying a boulder on my shoulder
for 40 days, nights and years...

The son of Moses,
literally, chosen to be frozen,
Alpha Male and golden
but only had Bros when...

It was convenient for them
to get the free come up,
but loyalty is earned
add it up and get your sum up...

I'm a King without a crown,
a Sire with no priors,
but if you dare to blow the smoke,
best believe I'll bring the fire...

THE JOURNEY PT. 2

If you only knew what God has done for me over these past few years. If you only knew the things that I've seen. If you only knew the experiences I've had to endure. If you only knew the strength that runs within me. If you only knew the wisdom I've acquired. If you only knew the things God has trained and prepared for me to do! If you only knew!

My journey is far from complete. My head is still bloody, but unbowed. I take joy in knowing what's in-store for me. It took time to understand that if you value yourself and what you are made of, how can you be upset when someone takes the value you have given? Whatever you put out into the universe will have an effect on someone or something at some point and time; and the ones who take will be accountable for using that value for good or evil.

Everything starts from within. Sometimes we must pull back from the distractions and focus on ourselves. We must look at how evolution effects each and every one of us. Some things and people never change and will continue to be who and what they are. It's your personal job to put yourself into a position to succeed. How we process things is up to us. How we digest and use those same things are determined by our growth and self-awareness. Your journey too, should start from within because without knowing yourself and loving yourself, you will not be able to truly give your productive self to someone else. Your family and loved ones deserve the best YOU that you can give. And you deserve the best YOU that you can be. Understand your journey. Research your journey... and it is then that you will be able to enjoy YOUR JOURNEY!

YOU'RE NOT READY

You were born,
like cheap corn,
that won't pop steady,
so if your seed don't respond to this heat,
you're not ready...

With no regard,
I discard all negative energies,
I've got a shield that won't let,
your venom get into me...

From early on I knew,
my mission was to inspire,
so I never aspired to desire
what other people acquired...

I see clearly
the things that are meant for me,
strong structure and raised up
to be what men were meant to be...

See, it's enough to go 'round,
it's the value your name brings,
you can love and support each other
even when you're doing the same thing...

Name just one King or one Queen
we all know plenty,
all under one God,
a God who loves many...

The son of Moses,
parting seas to make Gs,
and in the face of my enemy,
I won't stutter, cough or sneeze...

When you get off track,
I got your back, front and middle,
strong vibes for the weak
and Big Ups for the little...

My riddles and rhymes
don't define how I'm feeling,
like being Ride or Die,
don't make you cry
like I'm killing...

I'm building legacy
when I speak into existence,
all the blood and the tears
from perspiration and persistence...

Plant a seed, grow a tree,
that's how family flows,
never worry about defeat
'cause only family knows...

Your true destination
designed with you in mind,
long before your dreams
and the thoughts
you'll never find...

Focus and pause
in the storm remain steady,
and if your palms aren't facing the sky...
YOU'RE NOT READY!

FINISH THE RACE

I'm four years from 50,
had to learn to move swiftly,
top hat replaced the cap
a brotha looking more Nifty...

Though the eyes never missed me,
they're always watching my next move,
headliner of the show, yet
still forced to show and prove...

I don't read the news,
I have to live it every day,
double check my door locks
and where my child likes to play...

It's the American way
to always face competition,
ass-kissing for permission,
less praying, more wishing...

Hand over heart
like the Star-Spangled Banner,
a man with no manners
gripping my balls
to the banter...

They keep telling me
it's jealousy,
but how could that be,

I gave you the best of my life
and we know that ain't free!

I'm just an open book,
thru the stares and the looks,
I've kept your secrets safe,
from the pick pockets and the crooks...

I've always played the Rook
in the corner against the border,
observing moves of the fools,
every habit, action and order...

All to stay above water,
I was the paddle to your boat,
in the cold I kept you warm
I was more valuable than your coat...

But my spirit is strong,
I've been wronged for so long
thinking life is a musical
and every breath a sweet song...

My back has been the bridge
between many new friends
and once the need gets fulfilled
the disrespect is unreal...

So I chill,
deep breath... strong face,
just me in my space,
it matters not who you pass
but how you finish the race...

WORD PLAY

I'm just trying to find my purpose
on purpose
I seek and find,
perpetrators disguised as haters,
with curtains that leave you blind...

Teach and grind
for the knowledge
take a step back like Harden,
try to grow and cultivate,
before exposing my Secret Garden...

Never starving for attention
some just gotta have that,
but you can have that,
just pile my stocks like Nasdaq...

That's facts...
I give you purpose in my verses,
nursing relations full of holes
while your ships sink beneath the surface...

No cursing,
we all know that's for fools,
oiling up nuts to get screwed
without the tools...

No foundation
no way to elevate,

or levitate to a state
that no man or woman can debate...

Now that's great,
like how a tiger roars in the jungle,
no hair but I invest my best
to stack bundles...

No wonder your shallow thoughts
stay in the gutters,
what matters shatters your window of pain,
no shutters...

All my brothers and sisters
need to unify,
before you and I die
split down the middle
like the Phi...

Signs define my greatness,
created a legacy while hated,
misunderstood but one day
all my work will be celebrated...

INNOCENT ADVENTURE

I lay my head to rest... Asleep.

My body screams for your touch...
It's like I know you, but I don't!
I want to be with you, but
I can't!
Are you really there?

Thoughts of you take me
through an emotional
rollercoaster of feelings
that only lead me back to
the stunned point that I
started from...
Who are you?

You arose from deep
within my mind and have
taken me through journeys
I can neither control nor
understand...

I feel your rhythmic
pulsations, 1, 3... 2, 4.

My heart beats faster as I become more connected to you.
I can taste your words.
I can feel the warmth of your inner soul.
I want to savor you as if you were my last meal.

I want to explore every crevice and curve of your body and
mind.
I want to dance in your daily thoughts and build a home in
your heart.

I want to hear your inner voices speak to mine and
feel your warmth as you melt me like chocolate over a flame!

I want you to know me,
know my name,
know my heart.

I will wait for you...

I want my voice to soothe you to sleep. I won't be upset.
I want to cradle you with a love that you've never
experienced before so, that when you awake, you'll know you
are where you always wanted to be.

Is it time?
Is our Innocent Adventure coming to fruition?

My heart raises and my senses heighten.
Sweat pours off my back and drenches the sheets.
I awaken drunk from the aftertaste of your essence.

Our Innocent Adventure is now over.
I sleep, so that I can dream again!

PRAYER

GOD, I praise you because...

You are our Father, our Keeper, our Peace. I praise you for
sustaining us. I praise you for blessing us beyond our
knowledge and understanding. I praise you for writing the
chapters to our personal biographies. You are our author of
Life, Love, and eternal Salvation. I praise you for the seen
and unforeseen. You are our sight and our vision. Through
you, we are never blinded of your blessings. I praise you for
my paralleled path with my family and loved ones. I praise
you for placing me here with them. I praise you God for
knowing ALL things and for that, there is no need to worry
or fret. I praise you God for the past, present and future.

In the name of Jesus,

Amen

I NEED

I NEED...
I need my tears to fall without anger
I need my pain to hurt without fear
I need my release to come without repercussions
I need my loved ones to be near...

I need my haters to stand in the background
I need my enemies to bow down
I need my heart to heal now
I need my head to support my crown...

I need my destiny to be fulfilled
I need my doubters to take note
I need my life to shine brighter
I need my thoughts to have hope...

I need my hope to have purpose
I need my strength to be stronger
I need my weaknesses to disappear
I need my days to be longer...

I need my memories to be proud
I need my pride to be meek
I need my heart to take over
I don't need my mind to be weak...

I need my home to be at peace
I need the wolves to howl at a different moon

I need my emotional mind to have logic now
I need my heart to beat a different tune...

I NEED...

I need a friend who doesn't judge
I need my visions to take flight
I need a strong wind to blow
I need the fog removed from my sight...

I need peace under pressure
I need answers for my confusion
I need God to forgive me for my thoughts
I need to stop the self-abusing...

I need my mind to let go of what it can't control
I need my inner strength to rejoice
I NEED TO SAVE MY SOUL!!

SEEK PEACE

Seek peace, love, and happiness in life! Find your own road to your destination and your definition of success. Stop listening to people who've somehow become scholars because they could shoot a basketball, throw a football, or hold a microphone. If this isn't your lane, how can you see yourself being them? Don't allow someone to make their definition of success yours. Hard work is hard work in whatever profession or journey you choose. Money can't define you. Nowhere in the Bible does it say, "Thou shalt chase paper for the rest of his days." If your definition of success is money, then rethink things. What makes you happy? What brings you peace? What brings you love? Most of the people who boast about money don't really want you to have it because they would no longer have that advantage over you. You may not hold them in the same regard. That's part of the problem. We want equality but don't look at our equals the same. Everyone wants to be on a higher tier than the next. Be wise with your eyes and smart with your heart. There's a big difference in showing success and sharing success. Your peace is your peace and what is meant for YOU will be yours.

I AM ME

Sunshine, promise, praise the day…
As my head slowly rises from the pillow,
Gratitude fills me.

My lungs release confidence and purpose,
My mouth exhales a vapor of joy.

One foot follows the other in the direction of God's grace.
My face glows with exuberant energy and my eyes lock in on
my destination.

I am the vessel driven by my passionate soul.
I am the speed not limited by markers of time.
I embrace the moment to never be second to the seconds of
my life.

I rejoice in every memory that has molded me like a potter's clay.
Each experience shapes me.
I marvel at the image that is on display for all to see.

I AM ME!

I step over puzzle pieces that have fallen to the floor.
I am not complete, so I continue to move forward.
One foot in front of the other.

Good is the enemy of Great, so I continue to fit my pieces
together.
Molded, sculpted and radiant.

Just the way I want to be…

I AM ME!

8ATE

This is where I demonstrate
that I'm great
there's no debating...

Facts... just sit and wait
I levitate
to greater levels
while you hate ...

Let's get it straight
I fed you game
right off the plate...

Silver spoon
Golden grill
you showed up late
repelling fate...

Wait... welcome to the pearly gates
never forget to mention the dimension
where we're all praying to elevate...

Communication is the key
when you date
inebriating feelings
make you chill and relate...

To greater powers
that devour your mate
now get your weight up
'til your numbers equate...

Celebrate
drink it straight no chase
then get nourished
by the words you just ate...

1-2 - 1-8
birth date of
the greatest underrated
poet to narrate...

TALK TO HIM

My mind's racing impatiently
just wait and see
how the latency of my confessions
turn into blessings...

Keep pressing like hot combs
my shot roams
thru the night when you're not home
and pop domes...

Straight thru the cabbage
a savage
like a wildebeest
magnified the Reign for my son
until you feel the heat...

Nothings ever promised
be honest
that's a lie to me
every time you look in a mirror
you see a lot of me...

My mind is dope
like peeking thru kaleidoscopes
you can bite my style
but you can't swallow it
you'll choke ...

I was provoked
so let the last verse play
the first time I reign
will be your last worst day...

That's my genetic makeup
wake up from the drama
too many leaders chasing fame
too many followers chasing commas...

Imma state factuals
the actual things you need to hear
and if you think I'm being petty
well, that's the thing you need to fear...

I know you pay attention
and keep wishing that I fail,
but my gateway to heaven
will be the path that brings you hell...

MY ERA

I'm from that 'go get a switch'
and come right back,
that tough love era
had you ready to fight back...

Hot grits with the fish
was the way in the Port City,
sliding thru the streets late at night,
it was not pretty...

Now the game changed
like from tackle to two hand,
touch the wrong person
you get done up for two bands...

Money has no meaning,
I don't know why we fight for it,
whatever your profession
you be up late at night for it...

We call it evil
but that paper can change things,
the root of all goodness
but the evil remains seen...

Hard to keep the main thing
remaining the main thing,
mentality like a Mamba
is the venom the pain brings...

Same thing, different day,
when it's fun we all sound off,
and come up outta all of the Burroughs
like Groundhogs...

Another 6 weeks for the meek
when the sun out,
a brotha see a shadow
then he pulling his gun out...

We got one route
and that's usually the roundball,
that's also why we keep our young sons from around yawl...

Fast life,
we be trapping our own kind,
then get strapped to the life
and be capping to one time...

It's funny how these Prophets want profit
and coaches think they're philosophers,
they should stop it...

Play your lane
like we're running the relay,
'cause if I make you pause,
it's no guarantee on the replay...

And if I'm 'G'd' up,
tell me what's my bond worth,
why every clothier I know
dress like Fonzworth?

It's nothing new
but you swear it's official,
please don't take that Judas kiss
like they miss you...

EACH 1, TEACH 1

Each 1, Teach 1
we got goals to get,
I tried to reach you to teach you,
you turned and stole my shit...

Holy shit,
Art-thou-not-the-creator,
took 'da bait' just to argue 'bout
who's lesser or greater...

Laser cuts in your gut
should burn thru your equator
if you get full off bull,
you should still tip the waiter...

That's core
like abdominal 6 packs
while we Blacks out here
getting click-clacked
over Kit Kats...

It's gotta stop
'cause I already can't breathe
gotta mask but no cash
so they stealing life for free...

Quarantined,
they got me locked up
'*Akon*' man leading,

COVID 19 bullets screaming
and we can't stop the bleeding...

Already cued up
on the felt waiting to fall
chalk lines, no shot
just life behind the 8 ball...

They wanna mute our voice
but Tik Tok to our songs
while the clock for justice
been tick ticking too long...

Be strong fam,
not too strong 'cause they're scared,
you can die LIVE on camera
while your fam watch it get shared...

Be prepared for a change
Dimes & Nicks won't make you rich,
we'll continue to die like animals
until we mentally make that switch...

You out here making confessions
first learn ya lesson,
God saved YOU from ME
then saved me,
now that's a blessing...

Stressing over life don't seem right
but that's the nature,
handcuffed by the life,
Life's a Bi-yatch
you can't escape her...

Dying over flavors of paper
but you can't smoke these,
this the Last Dance,
be like Mike,
now that's some GOAT cheese...

JUST US

The whole problem with justice is
They don't trust us
It's just us, hands in the air
prepared to dust us...

OFF!

Lay the cloth over our face
With no remorse
Like a sport
They try to put us in holes
Par for the course...

I been searching for my path
All my life, God knows
but why my route have me fighting
More friends than foes...

Why's my culture a cult
Why's my history scarred,
Why can't I paint a perfect picture
Without stripes and bars...

STAND STILL

Don't even lie to me
you're trying to be
something that ain't even in your dichotomy …

It's gotta be
an easier way to become famous
but the real ones that put in the work
remain nameless…

You say you got it out of the mud
but you ain't worthy
when the pain came the rain stains
just left you dirty…

I heard he had an ego
but we know pride is fragile
when your strength broke like glass
you formally became casual…

People setting their clocks for 11:11
and saying they're blessed
while I'm grinding 24/7 around the clock
and steadily stressed…

So what's next?
cause angels fly & doves do cry
eyes see truth still
and mouths do lie…

I try to keep it a 100
but it's obvious man will
get mad at YOU
when they're the ones
stuck in the stand still...

I WALKED A MILE

Today I walked a mile in my own shoes
I turned down the chatter
I blocked out the boos...

No rules, only views
just peace and harmony
wind flurries and no worries
about someone harming me...

Just me and my best friend
no one making suggestions
no dancing around the ring
no sparring sessions with depression...

And that's a lesson in itself
let go and just breathe
walk past the things that you want
run to the things that you need...

I don't have greed
but I have a hunger for success
I don't flaunt what I've got
but I'm blessed to have the best...

Not that money can buy
because that's a man-made value
I don't care about the shoes, the watches and what have
you...

I care about health
and the wealth of me and mine
and if I got it out the mud
Imma rinse it off until it shine...

What's mine is for me
and what's yours is see through
my mirror reflects MY greatness
I can't be or see YOU...

And when the winds of change
make it strange to call us friends
remember a man's will won't stand still
that behavior never wins...

Today I walked a mile
'till my soles wore out
but mind was awakened
until my soul poured out.

SOME PEOPLE

Some people really don't care about the grind
they only care about the shine
but talk a good game
but dim as coals in the mine...

I say what's on my mind
and you should too
but actions speak louder
I do things you just don't do...

Always talking about ballin
and posting, "Let's Get It"
Your Nu Nu is old news
By now, I've did it and quit it...

You think these words are about you
Forget it... that's expected
and if you do
I'll lose about 20 friends in 20 seconds...

But I'm eclectic
DEEP is the only way I delve
Remember, Hitler had over a million followers
Jesus only had 12...

Talking about what you got
popping bottles and pulling triggas
some of you seen a FEW BODIES
but never seen SIX FIGURES...

Grow up and get your dough up
We're all on different levels
I can blow up
I got dynamite AND a shovel...

Sneakers and watches
man, I got that too
you need to get a house or that old lady
and go live in that shoe...

I don't need you to agree
I don't need the co-signing
you cling to someone else
so basically, you're co-whining...

Rihanna told you
Shine bright like a diamond
but you have to hear the clock fam
it's all about timing...

I BEEN writing and rhyming
it's how I release from the chest
I don't need social media
to release all the stress...

I separate from the BS
like oil does from water
you fake to make the pack laugh
you're just back draft of the slaughter...

And I look at the pain
through a windowpane of shame
and bust the glass out the frame
sweep the pieces and take the blame...

See... I'm all about my actions
the before and the after
I'm not some imaginary Saint
or some Facebook Pastor...

I'm not some needy guy
I'm just the guy I am
I don't need you to like my post
I could really give a damn...

It might sound mean
sometimes it takes that for you to listen
seek knowledge for yourself
you can keep praying or keep wishing...

I don't believe in having haters
that's just admission of defeat
haters are like pigeons
I'm just dropping bread for you to eat...

THE GOOD FIGHT

I fought the good fight
swung and kissed him good night,
I tried to spark change
to bring the hood light...

Nothing changed, same cycle
like 2 wheels spinning,
all that grinning turns to frowns
as soon as they see another winning...

I see it because I'm savvy
not savage and never petty,
every step I take is charged,
I guess I'm EverReady...

I tried to be a loyal friend,
we all deserve certain chances,
but when I'm quiet just understand
you don't know my circumstances...

I fought the good fight,
did exactly what I was told,
knew when to pocket my pride
and knew when to be bold...

But that story gets old
too many lies and insults,
we want the bag and happiness
that's the only results...

Big dream chasing,
embracing how could I eclipse these,
plots with 3 shots
or 3 dots like ellipses...

Goals over fame,
make a name, remain the same,
never expect a change in others
and for that blame the game...

It's strange... I'm strange
but knowing self is the key,
I've unlocked doors and walked in places
I was never supposed to be...

But I'm poured like concrete
soft impressions leave you stuck in,
your tracks without the facts
and that's a hard place to be tucked in...

Never gave a f*ck when
I was surprised or criticized,
and now when each day ends
our potential is minimized...

Trust me on this,
all things in life are not sweet,
be careful of the love you deny
and the new people you meet...

Greed lives across the street
and Envy is next door,
Jealously peeks through windows
and Hate seeps through the floor...

But what's in store is much greater
God's Plan... God's Man,
I fought the best fight I could,
now it's all in God's Hands...

BLUE ENVY

I got loose screws
a few tools
but no mechanic
shoot you a text
or shoot thru ya
if I'm feeling manic...

Never panic
I still got my wits about me
but I keep a list of you jits
who popping shit about me...

When the sun shines... I'm fine
but when it rains
the pour bores me
bottom line
Imma still shine in all my glory...

So, the moral of the story...
be careful what you ask for
don't wake the giant
then wonder what he kicked your ass for...

I'm humble but won't settle
hand on the metal if I need it
my passion growls like a belly in the night
so I feed it...

My prototype shines bright
no shade and no dimming
I'll stand in the Grand Limelight
and crush your lemon...

Just say Hi to the bad guy
we'll never see eye to eye
'cause when I spy envy...
just defriend me...

Defend your honor
that's if you even got any,
every deck gotta Joker
and jokes you got plenty...

The more you show what you got
the more we're on to the fronting
I can't tell if you ballin
or just never had nothing...

Just a lame move
you want your peers to idolize
all that generating of envy
is the same reason your idols died...

I despise guys that show their wives goods
low self-esteem
pretending that Life's good...

My track record Usain
years I trained for the finish
the more my value rises
the more I see yours diminish...

What the mirror sees
is what I'll already be
I don't need to brag on the things that people can already
see...

Blue Envy

AWAKE

My eyes part to sun rays breaking into my window.

The volume increases in my ears of birds chirping and lawn mowers rumbling.

Soon all senses are recognizable. I swing my feet onto the floor and gently stretch the remaining slumber away.

A new day has begun!

Thoughts race while schedules play table tennis inside my brain. I reach for my obsession and sprinkle media updates on my plate.

My thoughts and love travel to every loved one's door.

Morning showers of love.

Awake. Restored. Excited. Anxious. Blessed.

Thank God for another day never before seen.

COLD MORNINGS

Bed covers pressed against my earlobes,
body nestled and spun into a warm cocoon.

Toes wiggle, eyelids blink
But I don't wanna move

The air feels like razor blades cutting against my skin.

I slide down deeper in my cocoon and anticipate the buzz of
my alarm.

A warm leg crosses mine and heats my inner soul... Snooze
button.

Embraced in temporary warmth and permanent love;
wrapped in a glove under air that is well conditioned.

The count of the threads is the excuse in my head. At least
that's what I'm professing.

I'm seeking heat like a missile from every exposed portion of
my skin.

The TV remote is too far to reach so decisions need to be
made.

The covers form a tent over my head that morph into my
chambers.

I negotiate for time like a trial lawyer but the judge in my brain rules against me.

All rise. Verdict in. Time to conquer the day.

MY SHOULDERS

Strong, broad, and comforting.
A baby's pillow.
A crier's muzzle.
A nightstand to sit your problems on.

My shoulders…

Shrug off nonsense and
deflect punches.

Rolling… they are
defense.
Cold… they are
unforgiving.

When you upset me, they
carry my stress and knot
and ache.

Round yet sharp!
Sometimes used as a
weapon to jar you to the
ground.

They have endured and
inflicted pain. Like a ball
and chain, their whip can
cause damage.

Upright and straight, they can carry twice their weight.

My shoulders…

I press on and press up to strengthen them, but they still slump when I am sad.

GOOD rests on one, BAD on the other. They keep me even.

A frame for beautiful skin and immaculate flesh. Flirting hands and playful fists both aim at the same target.

A place of intimacy, counseling, privacy, and safety. Never closed to friends when they need a place to lean.

My shoulders…

Endure life's struggles and all its glory.
Draped under an invisible cape that can only tell half their story.

MASTER PLAN

Thinking of a master plan
With tears in my eyes
And forehead in my hand

I get the picture
But I was framed
By the games people play
And I refrain to name names
Or do the same as people say

I'm different!!!

In the mirror
I'm clearer than before
I worked to remove the smudges
endured the pain to restore

My reputation, my pride
My OUT-look from IN-side
Yeah, I be tripping sometimes
but took that bumpy ride in stride

I lied to myself
saying the road wasn't hard
Like lifting myself off the ground
Wouldn't leave my knuckles still scarred

I try to remember the bigger picture
But it's the small things that matter

Like how my confident swagger
Makes me the topic of chatter

Never knowing my story
But they all know my name
A fool to think my now and then
Are still one in the same

To have friends
One must show themselves to be friendly
But mistaking kindness for weakness
Brought me more enemies

So I took a deeper look
How do opposites attract
How does this heart in my chest
Place a bullseye on my back

So I react when attacked
I speak my own truth
Wearing my pride like a vest
Thinking I was bulletproof

The blame game has never given
A 1st place ribbon
It's just a disguise for the lies
And insecure life that you're living

Thanks for giving love
I could feel the passion burn
But we never learn that what's received
Should be given in return

And once the tables turn

It leaves us spinning in the air
On life's Ferris Wheel
Proving that life ain't a fair

But we press on like stickers
Looking to trigger our moment
Holding the master plan all the while
It's just we never own it...

REFLECTIONS

Lord… I thank you for the year that you've brought me
through
it was tough and sometimes painful
but as a man, I grew…

My heart has endured things
that my brain could not perceive
and in those times when
friends changed
I knew it was YOU who
would not leave…

Sometimes it's hard to be
thankful
for the things we cannot
see
it's even harder to be the
person
that you want us to be…

But because I am FREE
I know I'll always have
your hand
to lift me up as a man
and give me strong legs to
stand…

Lord, I thank you for the
essence

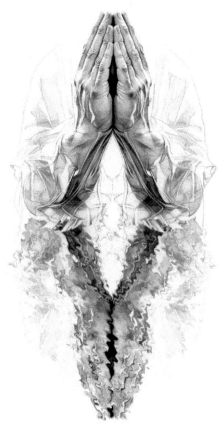

of what life is about
and may you judge us by our hearts
and not what comes from out our mouth...

I thank you for my kids
and the love I'm able to give
and although many will never share that love
for it I'd give my rib...

I thank you for the lives
that passed from us this year
for the joy their existence brought to us
and how it taught us not to fear...

And we know we make mistakes
but you still allow our hearts and souls to rest
even as we know we cannot live for you
when we're living in the flesh...

At best, I'm just a man
who gives life all he's got
as I learn that friends will come and go
whether we 'LIKE' it or not...

So I pray that you give us hope
and allow our spirits to move on
and look forward to your gracious light
through the dusk and the dawn...

And each year that grows near
I'll continue to thank you for what you do
for my friends, for my family
and all of my crew...

We cannot see the future
and we will not complain nor fuss
as we turn from past to present
God continue to be good to us!

Amen

PERSPECTIVE

The best part of my morning is waking up realizing that God did it again! He woke me up to see another day. The second-best part is feeling the internal, gravitational pull of love between me and my family members and loved ones. Internal peace and happiness are all I desire. To wake with no guard rails, ties, or hitches. We shouldn't owe social media a daily morning post to stay in the 'algorithm' that says we're relevant. We shouldn't have to show the world how much we're enjoying life while we're trying to enjoy it. To be comfortable knowing that my personal exploits are personal is golden. The more we try to show people we're winning, the more people envy our moves, duplicate our actions, and secretly wish for you to lose… all while simultaneously liking your post or intentionally scrolling past it.

Freedom starts with perspective …

WHO AM I?

The question is... Who Am I?

Do I even know myself?
Am I just a lost boy
who knows neither poverty nor wealth?

Being captured between self,
and who I want to be,
somehow it fogs the visions of the truths inside of me.

The realities of life that burn inside like hot coals and cabin
fires,
cause me to wonder why,
if we know our beliefs, are so many of us liars?

Who Am I, really?

Armani suits or Timberland boots?
An intelligent man or society's puppet
being strung away from my roots?

A scholarly voice and business suit does not make me more
the man.
If I chose to speak with a ghetto tongue,
does it mean my mind can't expand?

So who then am I living for?
society or my maker?

Must I go through life impressing those who live their lives as fakers?

My heart knows that I am very real to whatever is real to me, and as long as I am comfortable about myself
... that is Who I Am to be!

SOMEWHERE

Somewhere…
A person is dying.
A child is crying but no one seems to care.
A bird is singing.
An alarm is ringing, telling naive souls to beware…
Somewhere…
A candle burns.
A lonely heart yearns for the touch of a gentle hand.
A flower dies.
A woman tries to re-open her heart to another man …
Somewhere …
Rain brings love.
Showers from above rinse away pain and misery.
A man is sad.
A relationship has gone bad because future can't escape history…
Somewhere …
A world is at peace.
ALL violence has ceased, and no eyes ever shed a tear.
Somewhere…
Everyone loves each other.
All our sistas and brothas
Somewhere… SomeWHERE… Why not HERE?

OUR LOVE

From the very first day I met you
I saw the beauty in your soul
I never would have imagined
how this present would unfold…

You were the torch that lit my darkened path
the sun that warmed my day
YOU… renewed my inner flames
it was for YOU I prayed…

Your smile brings me happiness
your happiness gave me joy
your hand in marriage was a gift from God
that no one can destroy …

Our love is like an armor
our security & our shield
our love is destined to grow
like flowers in the fields…

Our love is like a romantic book
that we open and turn the page
and enjoy the chapters of loving words
that only get better with age…

Our love is a canvas
painted with brush strokes of life
a piece meant for display
in a museum of husband and wife…

Weeks to days and days to months
it feels our lives have just begun
I embrace our lives that are intertwined
Our bond, our love... Year One!

PARENTS

See me crawl, see me walk,
watch me strengthen, hear me talk...

See me play and run and laugh,
wipe away all evil from my path

Watch me grow
teach me,
beat me,
instill love in me,
never mistreat me

Help me learn right from wrong,
teach me patience when my roads are long

Teach me persistence
and tell me "I CAN"
Teach me how to be a father
as well as a man

Be there for me and help me provide,
make me see the difference between conceit and pride

Love me forever,
carry me through time,
watch me as I change
let me love all mankind...

Be there for me when I grow old,
help me remember the fond tales that were told.

Hear me laugh
see me cry
be there for me when we say goodbye.

A MOTHER'S LOVE

She wraps me in her loving arms,
a touch and love
so pure,
a mother's heart is
made of gold,
in sickness, she's
the cure...

Through days of
joy and nights of
fear,
Her voice is a
warm embrace,
she's always there
with love and care
written over her
face...

She guides us with
concern,
through pain,
through storm or
strife,
with strong advice and wisdom
that somehow blesses my life...

Her sacrifices are silent but grand,
a sheltering rock grounded in the sand.

In laughter shared
and tears wiped dry,
a mother's wisdom
pushes you to try...

She's always there to keep us safe,
she provides a happy home,
she gives without expecting back,
her love is always shown...

Her eyes sparkle like diamonds
that light the daunting nights,
a mother is our compass in life,
she keeps our goals in sight...

Endless love as deep as the sea,
as long as a country mile,
a mother's love is what everyone needs,
a blessing to every child...

HEY DADDY...

Hey Daddy,
It's been several months since you left,
I'm trying hard to do my part,
you told me, "Don't overstep..."

My boundaries
but I can't say life is
good
all around me,
I'm feeling lost and still
don't know
in what condition they
found me...

Day to day, I still pray
not on my knees but I lay,
staring at the ceiling
with these feelings that just won't go away...

Some things have changed
but it's the same as all our past conversations
some just don't get it
so, I quit with all those past complications...

I still have questions,
because you always had the answer,
I drug'em out over time
but time took away the chance to...

Dig beneath the layers of your mind,
it was priceless,
your words were life, but since you left
I'm the one feeling lifeless...

I still recite your favorite sayings,
I meet you when I'm dreaming,
I see you beaming from the clouds
I know that God's redeeming ...

Power... I'm glad he brought me a sign,
by design our bond was the kind
that most father's sons just don't find ...

I'm grateful
but it's been testing my faith to learn this lesson,
that I'll pass down to my son
'cause being a father is a blessing...

You told me
never let them take away ME,
I'm just trying to be
all that you thought I would be...

I see the rainbows when it rains
and all the pain from the sorrow,
it makes sense by end of day but then
here comes tomorrow...

A new day we've never seen
with a dream and new beginnings,
I bet you're fishing with a reel made of gold
with all your winnings...

Hey Daddy…

I'll keep on walking this line that you were toeing
because in this world, we're never knowing
Until then
I'll keep on going…

Although it's hard
and I feel so lost without you,
you know your family's caring for each other
and we couldn't do that without you!

PRAYER

Heavenly Father, who is the head of my life. Show up and walk through my house. Rebuke and bind all things that are not of you. Cancel assignments and terminate contracts that come against me and those I love! Take away all my worries, all illnesses and pain. Continually bless my job, and my finances. Continue to watch over my family and comfort my friends. Make me more like you and less like me.

In Jesus' name,

Amen

ABOUT THE AUTHOR

R. Steven Holmes (Steve) was born and raised in Wilmington, North Carolina. An athlete and artist from grade school through college, he started writing poetry and short stories for the college magazine. In his early twenties, he wrote lyrics and pursued a rap career. His love for sports and mentorship led him to coach youth football for sixteen years.

Steve graduated from East Carolina University with a major in Information Systems. With an insatiable appetite for conquering challenges, Steve was a member of the East Carolina football team and an initiate of the Eta Nu Chapter of Alpha Phi Alpha Fraternity, Inc. He has used his artistic talents to design book covers and starred in an online movie series. He is a software engineer, and also the founder and owner of Reign4ever clothing line (www.reign4ever.com), a brand he created to teach his sons entrepreneurship. They emphasize LIFE and LEGACY through sharing, caring and inspiring others.

Steve's passion for writing, music, design, and coaching is an inspiration to the people's lives he's positively impacted. Steve currently lives with his family in North Carolina.